PRO WRESTLING LEGENDS

CHELSEA HOUSE PUBLISHERS

PRO WRESTLING LEGENDS

Vince McMahon Jr.

Kyle Alexander

Chelsea House Publishers
Philadelphia

Produced by Chestnut Productions and Choptank Syndicate, Inc.

Editor and Picture Researcher: Mary Hull
Design and Production: Lisa Hochstein

CHELSEA HOUSE PUBLISHERS

Editor in Chief: Sally Cheney
Associate Editor in Chief: Kim Shinners
Production Manager: Pamela Loos
Art Director: Sara Davis
Director of Photography: Judy L. Hasday

Cover Photos: Sports Action
                  and Jeff Eisenberg Sports Photography

The Chelsea House World Wide Web site
address is http://www.chelseahouse.com

First Printing

1 3 5 7 9 8 6 4 2

Library of Congress Cataloging-in-Publication Data

Alexander, Kyle.
     Vince McMahon Jr. / Kyle Alexander.
        p. cm. — (Pro wrestling legends)
     Includes bibliographical references (p.) and index.
     ISBN 0–7910–6444–1 (alk. paper) — ISBN 0–7910–6445–X (pbk. : alk. paper)
        1. McMahon, Vince—Juvenile literature. 2. Wrestlers—United States—
     Biography—Juvenile literature. [1. McMahon, Vince. 2. Wrestlers.] I. Title. II.
     Series.

     GV1196.M43 A44 2001
     796.812'092—dc21
     [B]
                                                                              00–069392

Contents

1   A HOUSE DIVIDED

They had always been a close family . . . until now. As close as they were before, that's how far apart they had become.

Vince McMahon Jr. stood in one corner. Linda McMahon, his wife, stood in another corner. Shane McMahon, their oldest child, stood in a third corner. Stephanie McMahon, their daughter, stood in a fourth corner. The event was Wrestle-Mania 2000 on April 2 at Arrowhead Pond in Anaheim, California, and the McMahons were a house divided.

Stephanie was in Triple-H's corner. She had married him months earlier and was there to help him win the World Wrestling Federation (WWF) World heavyweight title.

Shane was in Big Show's corner. Big Show had returned to the WWF in February to get revenge against the Rock, and had enlisted the young McMahon's help.

Linda was in Mick Foley's corner. Foley (whose ring name is Mankind) had retired from the federation earlier in the year, but Linda had brought him back so that she could stake her claim in the family's power struggle.

And Vince McMahon Jr., whose family's involvement in wrestling stretched back to the early 1900s, was in the Rock's corner. He was enraged at his daughter for marrying Triple-H,

---

Shane McMahon and the Big Show face off against Stephanie McMahon and her husband Triple H in a battle for control of the federation.

and he wanted to establish firm control of the federation.

The sellout crowd at the Pond watched in nervous anticipation as the four unlikely couples made their way to the ring. Sure, the Rock's world title was at stake in this "Fatal Four-Way Match," but the McMahon soap opera was more interesting than any athletic battle. Clearly, the McMahons were the most dysfunctional family in wrestling.

After the bell rang, the four combatants battled inside and outside of the ring while the McMahons and the fans watched. With four minutes gone, Foley clocked the Big Show over the head with a chair. Seconds later, the Rock pounced on top of the Big Show to score the pin. The Big Show had been eliminated.

Only three wrestlers and three McMahons remained. Triple-H tried to convince Foley that it was in their best interests to double-team the Rock. Foley, however, wanted to fight this battle on his own terms. With more than 10 minutes gone in the match, Foley stunned Triple-H with a DDT (a move in which one man grabs his opponent around the neck in the crook of his arm, then, using a swift sitting-down motion, drives the opponent's head into the mat), then locked his "mandible claw" finishing hold on Triple-H. The Rock whipped Triple-H with the championship belt. Foley turned and clamped the mandible claw (a move that finds Mankind literally reaching into his opponent's mouth to paralyze him) on the Rock, who fought his way out of the lethal hold. Foley retained the advantage and battered Triple-H and the Rock.

But the Rock fought back. He DDT'd Foley for a two-count, then recovered from a double-teaming effort by Triple-H and Foley. Now it was every man for himself. The action moved outside the ring. Foley picked up the metal steps leading to the ring and dropped them on the Rock's head, then he smashed the Rock through a ringside table. Foley went through the table, too, and lay motionless on the floor. Triple-H dragged Foley back into the ring and scored the pin. Now only Triple-H and the Rock remained, along with Stephanie and Vince McMahon.

Foley returned to the locker room, but stormed back moments later carrying a base-

The Rock was furious when he realized that Shane McMahon and his family had collaborated to ensure he would lose the WWF World heavyweight title to Stephanie McMahon's husband Triple H.

ball bat wrapped in barbed wire. He swung the bat over his head, then brought it down on Triple-H again and again. Triple-H fought off the attack and slammed the Rock into the metal steps with a piledriver, a move in which one man holds his opponent upside-down and slams his head into the mat—or in this case, a piece of steel.

The scene was one of utter chaos: The Rock and Triple-H fought into the crowd. The Rock sent Triple-H through the announcers' table. Vince interfered on the Rock's behalf, but Shane McMahon returned to the ring and hit his father with a TV monitor. Vince couldn't believe what his son had done. Vince and Shane continued to fight as the Rock and Triple-H lay nearly unconscious in the middle of the ring. Vince, with blood gushing from his forehead, stumbled back to the locker room. The Rock DDT'd Triple-H.

The match appeared to be over, but Shane still had something to say about the outcome. He picked up a metal chair that was lying in the ring. His intention was to hit the Rock, but the Rock turned and whipped Triple-H into the chair. Triple-H fell to the mat. The Rock prepared to pounce on top of Triple-H for the pin. The crowd rose to its feet in anticipation.

Then Vince returned to the ring. He picked up the chair and struck Shane, then he smashed the Rock with the chair. One more chair shot by Vince later, Triple-H covered the Rock for the pin and the world title.

Furious, the Rock attacked both Stephanie and Vince. He had been victimized by a devious plot: Shane, Vince, and Stephanie had been in cahoots all along. The next night at *Raw Is War*,

Vince proclaimed his hatred for the Rock, and hugged Stephanie and Shane.

Once again, as they had for decades, the McMahon family ruled wrestling.

THE McMAHON LEGACY

The history of the McMahon family is the history of ring sports in the 20th century. Jesse McMahon, Vince Jr.'s grandfather, promoted wrestling and boxing matches in the early decades of the century. He promoted boxing with the legendary Tex Rickard, who built Madison Square Garden in New York in 1925 and founded the New York Rangers of the National Hockey League.

Jess McMahon graduated from Manhattan College and was known as a hard-working man who put his family first. In those days, promoters in the fight game were stereotyped as cigar-smoking, card-playing, hard-talking "men's men" who would do anything to make a buck. Jess McMahon's main concern was being out of the office by five o'clock so that he could go home to his family in Far Rockaway on Long Island. He owns a permanent part of sports history: On December 11, 1925, he promoted the first boxing card at the old Madison Square Garden. The event featured a light heavyweight championship bout between Jack Delaney and Paul Berlenbach.

Vince McMahon Sr.—Jess's son and the man who would become Vince Jr.'s father—grew up in the smoke-filled arenas typical of those days. In an article in *Wrestling World* magazine,

---

Vincent Kennedy McMahon Jr. worked as a salesman and a day laborer before his father gave him a chance to prove himself in the wrestling business. He quickly surpassed everyone's expectations.

Vince Sr. recalled those exciting, happy days of his childhood:

"My big charge came from seeing Ching Johnson of the Rangers come up the ice with the puck," Vince Sr. said. "He was electric, shedding body checks like [football superstar] Bronko Nagurski shaking off tacklers."

Vince Sr.'s way with words made him perfect for the job of wrestling promoter. In 1935 Vince Sr. promoted his first wrestling card. Twenty-one years later, on November 26, 1956, Vince Sr. promoted his first wrestling card at Madison Square Garden, but only 10,400 fans showed up to see heavyweight champion Antonino Rocca battle Dick the Bruiser. Three months later, however, the Garden was sold out for the tag team main event of Rocca and Verne Gagne battling Hans Schmidt and Karl Von Hess. The Garden quickly became the Mecca of pro wrestling in the glory years of the late 1950s and 1960s.

Back in the late 1950s the WWF didn't exist, and the National Wrestling Alliance (NWA) was the dominant federation in North America. But in late 1962 and early 1963, trouble developed. Buddy Rogers had been NWA World champion since June 30, 1961. Promoter Toots Mondt controlled Rogers's title defense schedule and rarely let him defend the title outside the Northeast. That upset promoters in other parts of the country. On January 24, 1963, Rogers lost the world title to Lou Thesz. The next day, Vince Sr. founded Capitol Sports Corporation, otherwise known as the World Wide Wrestling Federation (WWWF), in Washington, D.C. Rogers became the WWWF's first world champion, though he held the title for only a short time.

Bruno Sammartino defeated Rogers on May 17, 1963, and went on to dominate the WWWF with two world title reigns totaling 11 years.

By this time, Vince McMahon Sr. had an 18-year-old son. Vincent Kennedy McMahon Jr. was born in Pinehurst, North Carolina, on August 24, 1945. He did not have an easy childhood and wouldn't meet his biological father until he was 12 years old.

"I immediately fell in love with him," Vince Jr. told *Icon* magazine. "I wanted to be just like him."

By Vince's own admission, his childhood couldn't have been any more troubled. His mother was on her fifth husband. His stepfather regularly beat him up. He grew up in a trailer park. As a result of his dyslexia, Vince Jr. had difficulty reading. Vince Jr. caused so much trouble that his mother sent him off to a military academy. According to an article in *Talk* magazine, Vince Jr. was the first cadet in the history of Fishburne Military School in Virginia to be court-martialed.

"What I learned as a kid was simple," said Vince Jr., who has always been reluctant to talk about his childhood. "If I lived through it, I won. And I just kept living through it. One good thing about the way I grew up is that I had no limitations, no rules. I have no fear of failure."

Vince Jr. met his future wife, Linda, in a North Carolina church when she was 13 and he was 16. They got married in 1966, when he was 21 and she was 18.

"I promised Linda two things when I married her," Vince told *Icon*. "I promised I'd always love her, and I always have. And I promised her never a dull moment."

McMahon graduated from East Carolina State University in 1968 with a degree in business administration. By that time, he was begging his father to let him into the wrestling business, but Vince Sr. wanted his son to be an accountant or a lawyer. Instead, Vince Jr. sold paper cups and encyclopedias. Vince and Linda moved to Maryland, where he continued selling cups.

"I thought there must be more to life than selling cups," Vince said to *Icon*. "So I quit."

Linda gave birth to their first child, Shane, on January 15, 1970. Vince started working 16-hour days as a laborer. He kept calling his father, begging for work in wrestling. Finally, in 1971, Vince Sr. relented and made his son head of Capitol Wrestling's operations in Bangor, Maine. The job came with a warning: If you're successful, great. If you're not, you're out of the business.

"It was a real struggle to convince my dad to let me work with him," Vince Jr. told *Talk*. "My dad was more conservative than I am, and he didn't want me in the business because at the time it was very much a kind of feast-or-famine deal. But from the beginning I longed for his business, for those larger-than-life characters and that show-business theatricality."

Vince, Linda, and Shane moved to Connecticut, where Vince and Linda worked out of their home. She managed the office. He drove back and forth to Maine, piling up miles on the family car. Much to his father's surprise, Vince was successful in Maine. He seemed to have a flair for promotion and for using television to advertise upcoming cards. After proving himself in Bangor, Vince Jr. was given responsibility for all of Capitol's operations in New England. Then came Vince Jr.'s big break. One day Vince Sr. fired his TV announcer shortly before the show was going to go on the air. He needed somebody to take over.

"I'll do it," Vince Jr. said, seizing the opportunity.

Throughout the 1970s Vince Jr. became famous as the face and voice of the WWWF. As the play-by-play man for WWWF telecasts, Vince Jr.'s face was the first thing viewers saw when they tuned in to wrestling every Saturday morning and evening. Perhaps best of all, Vince Jr. got to make up for lost time with his father.

"I think those were the greatest days of his life, when he finally got the chance to develop a

Vince and Linda McMahon took a huge chance in 1982 when they agreed to buy Capitol Wrestling Corporation, but their hard work and farsighted thinking paid off. Together they built an entertainment empire.

true relationship with his father," WWF announcer Jim Ross told *Icon*.

Vince Jr.'s deep voice and his trademark gesture of raising an eyebrow any time rule-breaking managers like Capt. Lou Albano, the Grand Wizard of Wrestling, and "Classy" Fred Blassie threatened an opponent, became a hallmark of WWWF broadcasts. But Vince Jr. had bigger plans than simply being an announcer and head of the WWWF's New England base. In fact, he had bigger plans than his father had ever dreamed.

In 1979 Vince Jr. and Linda bought the Cape Cod Coliseum. They used the building not only for wrestling matches, but for rock concerts, sporting events, and other entertainment events. Vince Jr. and Linda learned the ins and outs of promoting live events and selling souvenirs. In 1980 they formed Titan Sports. He named himself chairman, and she named herself president.

A few years later, in 1982, Vince Sr. was getting tired of the business. He had spent over a half century promoting wrestling matches and was ready to retire. Vince Sr. wanted to sell the business, and Vince Jr. was worried that he would sell Capitol Sports to someone else. But Vince convinced his father and his father's business partners to sell Capitol Wrestling Corporation to him. He told his father that investors with significant financial resources backed him. That was a lie.

"Everyone wondered where the money was coming from," Vince Jr. recalled. "I wondered too! My father thought it was other people's money. It was a tremendous risk, but it was the only way I could do it."

Vince Jr. and Linda agreed to make four quarterly payments of about $250,000 each. If they missed a payment, the business would be returned to Vince Sr.'s business partners. Vince Jr. and Linda would lose all of their money. With this in mind, Titan Sports set out to change the face of wrestling in the United States.

"My dad never would have sold me the business had he known what I was going to do, for fear that I wouldn't live through it," Vince Jr. said.

Vince Jr. was about to challenge the establishment. He was about to say, "We're not doing things your way anymore. We're doing things my way."

His way was revolutionary.

3 BREAKING DOWN WALLS

In the early 1980s, all the wrestling federations in North America were regional. Though they had names like the "World" Wrestling Federation (WWF), the "National" Wrestling Alliance (NWA), and the "American" Wrestling Association (AWA), there was nothing worldly, national, or all-American about any of them.

The NWA was a loose association of local promotions, the strongest of which ran cards and aired TV shows in the Mid-Atlantic, Southeast, and Midwest. The WWF ran cards and broadcast TV shows in the Northeast. The AWA ran cards and aired TV shows in Minnesota and a few other states. Several small, regional federations filled in the open areas.

A look at two of the world championships of this era makes the localized nature of the sport clear. Through 1978 five of the first seven WWF World heavyweight title changes took place in New York, the other two occurred in Pennsylvania and Maryland. Through 1975 there were 18 AWA World title changes; 15 of them occurred in Minnesota.

Of course, there were no written rules that the federations couldn't invade each other's territories. Such rules would have been against federal anti-trust laws, which are designed to ensure competition. But there was no competition in

Vince McMahon stands in front of a poster of Hulk Hogan during a 1985 press conference. Hogan was the kind of colorful, exciting wrestler McMahon wanted to cultivate in his federation.

wrestling. All of the promoters had their own territory. They all minded their own business.

For this reason, it was unlikely that there was an NWA fan living in New York City or a WWF fan living in Atlanta. In 1981 and 1982 Bob Backlund was WWF World champion of a very small portion of the world, and Ric Flair was NWA World champion of another very small portion of the world.

"Essentially they had all these little fiefdoms set up, pretty much the way the Mafia would have its own territories divided by family," McMahon told *Talk* magazine, "and that meant you didn't go into someone's territory without serious repercussions from everyone."

As is usually the case, however, a lack of competition hurt the product the fans were buying. The weekly television shows were taped in small, dimly lit studios. There was little attention paid to production values, such as lighting and music. The heads of each federation had no incentive to improve their product because they didn't have to be better than anyone. The wrestling fans in each area had a choice: Watch the wrestling federation that ruled their territory or find another sport to watch.

In the early 1980s large numbers of wrestling fans were finding other sports to watch. Vince Jr., who had gambled his financial life on buying the WWF from his father, had no interest in owning a sinking business.

"There were only so many big cities in the Northeast," McMahon said, "so I had to go into these other territories. I wanted to take the business and position it where I thought it belonged, all the way in the mainstream.

I figured that the formula that worked in the Northeast would work everywhere else."

According to the late Gorilla Monsoon, a longtime TV announcer, "He [McMahon] didn't want to promote in 15 states, he wanted to promote in 15 countries."

Or more. First, however, McMahon had to knock down barriers in the United States. He went into television markets that previously had been the exclusive property of the NWA or the AWA, and he offered the stations money to broadcast his show, a business practice previously unheard of in pro wrestling.

"I banked on the fact that they [the other federations] were behind the times, and they were," McMahon said to *Fortune* magazine. "All of them."

WWF heavyweight champion Hulk Hogan faces off Andre the Giant at a New York press conference on February 3, 1988, to promote their upcoming match on The Main Event, *an NBC prime time special. The Hogan/ Andre bout was the first pro wrestling match aired on network television in 30 years.*

McMahon's formula was simple, and it made a lot of sense: He'd use WWF TV shows to hook fans in traditional NWA and AWA areas on the WWF, then he'd lure them to the federation's live arena cards. Naturally, the heads of the other federations were in an uproar, but they couldn't do anything to stop McMahon. After all, McMahon was competing. He wasn't violating any laws.

McMahon raised the standard for wrestling on TV by improving production values and camera angles and adding colorful graphics and bass-thumping rock 'n' roll music. Wrestlers were encouraged to wear outlandish outfits and say outlandish things. His goal was to turn wrestling into an entertainment extravaganza. He offered to buy out small federations. If they refused, he'd buy air time on the TV stations in their markets. Wrestling fans liked the entertainment he was providing. Before long, WWF wrestling broadcasts were airing in most major television markets throughout the country.

While he was expanding the WWF's television base, Vince Jr. set his sights on expanding the WWF's talent base as well. He eventually counted previously regional stars like Bret Hart, Randy Savage, Junkyard Dog, Ted DiBiase, Jack and Jerry Brisco, Lex Luger, Kerry Von Erich, and even Ric Flair, as WWF wrestlers, but his biggest signing came in late 1983, when he brought Hulk Hogan to the WWF.

Hogan was well known to serious wrestling fans. He had been in the WWF once before, in 1979, when he wrestled as a rulebreaker under manager Freddie Blassie. In 1982 he starred as a wrestling villain in the Sylvester Stallone movie *Rocky III*. In 1983 in Tokyo, Japan, he defeated Antonio Inoki to become the first International Wrestling Grand Prix champion. The widespread success Hogan desired, though, was escaping him. Almost ready to leave the sport entirely, Hogan nonetheless signed with the AWA in 1983.

McMahon knew that making the WWF more vibrant, colorful, and exciting meant more than improving television production. It meant bringing in exciting, colorful wrestlers who could capture the fans' attention. At the time, however, the WWF World champion was Bob Backlund, a bland, scientific wrestler with all-American looks and minimal personality.

The WWF needed a talent overhaul, and McMahon wanted that talent overhaul to start at the top with one of the biggest wrestlers in the world. Hogan was just what McMahon was looking for: a 6' 8", 275-pound mountain of muscle with long blond hair and comic book looks.

Hogan arrived in the WWF shortly after the Iron Sheik won the world title from Backlund on December 26, 1983. Because of an injury, Backlund was unable to wrestle in the rematch against the Iron Sheik on January 23, 1984, at Madison Square Garden. Hogan took his place, much to the dismay of several WWF wrestlers who had wanted the title shot. But Hogan proved he was worthy of the challenge by quickly dispatching the Iron Sheik to win the WWF World title.

"Hulkamania" was born, and a new era of professional wrestling began.

This should have been a great time for Vince Jr. He had achieved his dream of owning the WWF. Attendance and television viewership was rising, and people were noticing the changes in the WWF. Instead, it was a time of tragedy. On May 27,1984, Vince McMahon Sr. died.

Nobody knows how Vince Sr. would have reacted to how his son would change the business of wrestling. Who knows what Vince Sr. would have said if he was alive when his son bought Georgia Championship Wrestling, and, on July 14, 1984, took over the NWA's airtime on cable SuperStation WTBS's *World Championship Wrestling*. He probably wouldn't have been happy. Then again, Vince Sr. was the man who broke from the NWA in 1963 and formed the WWWF. Rebellion ran in the family.

Fans of the program *Georgia Championship Wrestling* were outraged when McMahon removed the NWA from WTBS and replaced it with WWF wrestling. Thousands of complaints poured in, but McMahon was defiant.

"We'll show these complainers the difference between a major league and a minor league production, given time," McMahon told a reporter for the *Atlanta Constitution*.

McMahon's purchase of Georgia Championship Wrestling meant that he was, in a way, a business partner with WTBS owner Ted Turner, who wasn't happy about having McMahon on board. *World Championship Wrestling* on Saturday nights was one of the highest-rated shows on TBS and all of cable. Turner fought back by offering blocks of programming time to other wrestling promoters. Eventually, the NWA regained its programming slots on TBS on Saturday mornings and evenings, and McMahon and TBS parted ways.

McMahon, however, didn't really need TBS. He was gaining national exposure in other ways. McMahon talked singer Cyndi Lauper and her boyfriend-manager David Wolff into appearing on WWF TV shows. They feuded with manager Capt. Lou Albano, who claimed he was running Lauper's career. The feud brought wrestling squarely into the mainstream of American popular culture. On February 18, 1985, MTV aired "The War to Settle the Score", a live bout pitting Hogan against "Rowdy" Roddy Piper. Hogan won by disqualification when Lauper and actor Mr. T interfered.

Lauper helped turn the WWF into a mainstream success. Suddenly, people who had never paid attention to wrestling were talking about Hogan, Piper, Albano, Lauper, and Mr. T. Lauper started using wrestlers in her videos. Everyone, it seemed, was talking about "the rock 'n' wrestling connection."

McMahon wasn't nearly finished changing the face of wrestling.

McMahon's idea was to create an event that would be wrestling's version of the Super Bowl. The greatest wrestlers would compete in the greatest matches, while celebrities from around the world watched from ringside. There would be musical acts, fireworks, and plenty of glitz and glamour. Fans would shell out big bucks to watch the event on closed-circuit TV.

The event was called WrestleMania.

WrestleMania I was held on March 31, 1985, at Madison Square Garden. The arena sold out in a hurry. Fans paid to watch the event from one of 135 closed-circuit television locations in 50 states and 24 countries. Cyndi Lauper was there. The famous piano player Liberace was there. Yankees manager Billy Martin was there. Boxing legend Muhammad Ali was a guest referee for the main event, in which Hulk Hogan and Mr. T defeated Roddy Piper and Paul Orndorff. The event was a raging success: McMahon brought in $12 million on WrestleMania I.

Success snowballed for the WWF. On April 29, 1985, Hogan appeared on the cover of *Sports Illustrated* magazine. The issue with Hogan on the cover was the second-best seller of the year for *SI*, right behind the swimsuit issue. On May 11, 1985, pro wrestling returned to network television for the first time in 30 years, when *Saturday Night's Main Event* premiered on NBC. In the main event, Hogan battled Bob Orton Jr. with Piper, Mr. T, and Orndorff at ringside.

The WWF continued to acquire top talent. Wrestlers realized that the WWF was the major

Boxer Muhammed Ali, left, was guest referee at Wrestle- Mania I on March 31, 1985, and he made the call when the team of Hulk Hogan and Mr. T defeated Roddy Piper and Paul Orndorff.

league of wrestling, the place where the spotlight of global fame shined brightest—and the money was the best to be had in the sport.

"It was like getting called up from A-ball to the major leagues," said "Macho Man" Randy Savage, a former professional baseball player who arrived in the WWF in 1985 and quickly became a superstar.

McMahon was ruthless as he steamrolled rival federations. He'd lure a top star from a federation by offering big money, then show up in that federation's territory a few months later with that top star wrestling in the main event. The NWA and AWA didn't know how to react. They were losing many of their top wrestlers— and many of their fans, too. Attendance was dwindling in the AWA, and it finally folded in 1990. The NWA probably wouldn't have survived, either, if stars such as Dusty Rhodes and Ric Flair hadn't remained loyal to the federation for so long, but even both of them ultimately defected to McMahon's WWF, if only for a brief while.

McMahon was not above criticism. Numerous national wrestling publications, particularly *Pro Wrestling Illustrated* and its family of magazines, criticized the WWF for being too much about glitz and glamour and not enough about wrestling. Hogan was considered a no-talent brawler who got by only because of his sheer strength. WWF TV shows were heavy on non-wrestling gimmicks, such as a segment in which wrestler Adrian Adonis dressed in outlandish pink outfits and interviewed and insulted his guests. On March 1, 1986, the WWF's first Slammy Awards were aired on MTV; wrestlers sang and performed skits.

Unusual awards, such as "Best Entrance Music," were handed out.

Criticism of the WWF mounted, but the money kept pouring in.

On April 7, 1986, WrestleMania II took place in three locations: Nassau Coliseum on Long Island, the Rosemont Horizon near Chicago, and the Los Angeles Sports Arena. The card was aired on pay-per-view TV to an international audience and once again was a raging success for the WWF. A year later, a North American live wrestling record crowd of 93,173 packed the Silverdome in Pontiac, Michigan, to watch Andre the Giant battle Hogan in the main event of WrestleMania III. That attendance record stands to this day.

McMahon had power, and he knew it. The first two WrestleManias had meant big money for cable television operators, so in November 1987, McMahon flexed his muscle. Since 1983, Starrcade had been the spotlight event on the NWA's annual schedule. Starrcade was always held on Thanksgiving. In 1987, for the first time ever, the NWA planned to air Starrcade on pay-per-view.

McMahon realized the NWA was on shaky ground. It was trying hard to play catch-up to McMahon and the WWF and had just spent millions to acquire the Universal Wrestling Federation (UWF) and its TV contracts. So McMahon came up with a new pay-per-view event called the Survivor Series. The show would be held on November 26, 1987—Thanksgiving Day.

Of course, cable television operators weren't happy with this arrangement. They would have preferred that the WWF and the NWA hold their big holiday events on different nights. McMahon, however, wasn't interested in appeasing the cable TV people. He was interested in making a power play. McMahon told the pay-per-view and closed-circuit TV vendors they had to choose between the two shows. If they wanted to carry Starrcade, they wouldn't get the Survivor Series. If they wanted to carry the Survivor Series, they couldn't carry Starrcade.

McMahon's gamble paid off. Most cable operators went with the proven product: the WWF. McMahon had taken an important step toward dominating the pay-per-view audience.

McMahon expanded the WWF's pay-per-view offerings in 1988. On March 27, 1988, WrestleMania IV was aired from the Atlantic City Convention Center. SummerSlam was added to the schedule on August 29. The second Survivor Series was held on November 24. McMahon even tried his luck in another sport. The WWF's first non-wrestling pay-per-view was a boxing match between Sugar Ray Leonard and Donny Lalonde on November 7, 1988. The event, however, was a commercial failure.

Still, the WWF's success could not be denied. On October 17, 1988, *Forbes* magazine reported that the WWF was worth an estimated $100 million. Vince Jr. was a rich man. But the world Vince McMahon had worked so hard to build was about to start crumbling down around him.

4 THE WORST OF TIMES

The WWF's cast of characters was unlike any the sport had ever seen. There was Ted DiBiase, who called himself the "Million-Dollar Man." DiBiase insisted that "everybody has his price," and sought to buy off wrestlers, referees, and titles. DiBiase would stuff money into the mouths of his opponents, then his bodyguard, Virgil, would retrieve the cash.

There was "Ravishing" Rick Rude, who wore skin-tight wrestling tights, gyrated his hips to music before matches, invited female fans into the ring for a kiss, and outraged countless people with his antics.

There was Koko B. Ware, who was always accompanied to the ring by his colorful parrot, and Jake "the Snake" Roberts, who carried a giant python to the ring and frequently unleashed it on his terrified opponents.

How about the Honky Tonk Man, the intercontinental champion whose motto was "I'm cool, I'm cocky, I'm bad." The Honky Tonk Man was an Elvis Presley impersonator who enjoyed serenading the fans with his guitar, even though the fans didn't want to hear him.

Owen Hart, one of the best all-around wrestlers in the world, was forced by federation promoters to don a blue mask

Critics protested that McMahon had turned the WWF into a three-ring circus, but fans loved the federation's bizarre cast of characters.

and a blue cape and wrestle anonymously as the Blue Blazer.

Fans detested Brother Love, the bogus evangelist who hosted interview segments on WWF telecasts and coined the phrase, "I luuuv yewwww!"

In the WWF occurrences that would have been outlandish anywhere else didn't seem too unusual. The Ultimate Warrior beat Bobby Heenan in a wrestling match, then stuffed him into a weasel suit. Heenan hopped around the ring like the Easter Bunny—just another match in the WWF.

The WWF, it seemed, would do anything to get attention.

"To me, wrestling in the WWF has become a pathetic circus," two-time former WWF World champion and pro wrestling legend Bruno Sammartino told *Pro Wrestling Illustrated* magazine. "Today you see this guy with the python snake, and the guy with the bird, and the dog. In my career, my ambition was to bring respect to professional wrestling. I feel that the WWF has made a complete 180-degree turn. I'm embarrassed to be associated with wrestling today."

Criticism of the WWF's inside-the-ring antics turned out to be the least of the federation's problems. As the 1990s began the WWF's problems started almost immediately. In August 1990 popular commentator Jesse Ventura left the federation because of a dispute over the use of his name and likeness on WWF merchandise. Ventura, who had been a commentator on almost every major WWF card for the past five years, was considered the main reason for the federation's success on television. Ventura sued the federation to recover royalties.

The biggest problems for the federation, however, were charges in the media and throughout the industry that its biggest and most muscular wrestlers were not only using steroids, but were encouraged to use them by the WWF. Steroids are illegal in the United States, and they can cause serious damage to those who use them.

On June 27, 1991, Dr. George T. Zahorian, a former ringside physician for WWF bouts in Pennsylvania, was convicted on 12 counts of selling anabolic steroids to four pro wrestlers and a weightlifter. During the trial, Zahorian testified that he had sold steroids to Hogan and McMahon, as well as to others. Hogan denied the charges.

The WWF responded with damage control. At a press conference three weeks later, McMahon admitted that he had experimented with steroids four years earlier, and he announced the federation's new drug testing policy: WWF stars would now undergo mandatory testing for steroids.

But the federation's actions did not live up to its promises. Testing didn't start until November 1991. The second round of tests wasn't taken until early 1992. Criticism of the WWF mounted.

Not that it hurt business. In 1990 McMahon's Titan Sports grossed $1.7 billion from licensed products. In the fall of 1991 the WWF signed eight-time NWA World champion "Nature Boy" Ric Flair, the man considered to be one of the greatest wrestlers in NWA/WCW history. Flair's defection was further proof that the WWF was the major league of wrestling. Three WWF pay-per-view events grossed a total of $49 million, more than any pop music specials or boxing matches broadcast on pay-per-view.

Still, the WWF's internal problems threatened to bring the federation to its knees. On March 2, 1992, WWF officials Pat Patterson and Terry Garvin resigned after several former WWF employees, including wrestler Barry Orton, charged them with sexual misconduct. Around the same time, former wrestler "Superstar" Billy Graham revealed that he had injected Hogan with steroids "hundreds of times." Hogan denied the charges. So did

McMahon, who refuted the charges of sexual abuse and denied that his wrestlers were abusing steroids.

Then WWF World champion Randy Savage appeared on the *Arsenio Hall Show* and admitted to having experimented with steroids when they were legal.

Not that all news was bad news for the WWF. In January 1993 the WWF celebrated the return of live (sometimes) televised wrestling to prime time television with the debut of WWF *Monday Night Raw* on cable's USA Network. The show, which at first was aired from small arenas such as the Manhattan Center in New York, was an instant ratings hit. And McMahon got his first taste of inside-the-ring action when he and several other WWF stars interfered in some of Jerry Lawler's matches in Memphis, costing Lawler the United States Wrestling Alliance (USWA) heavyweight title.

McMahon's feud with Lawler was never settled, because he was too busy battling his legal opponents. On November 18, 1993, a federal grand jury indicted McMahon and Titan Sports on charges of possession of anabolic steroids and conspiracy to distribute anabolic steroids. If convicted, McMahon faced eight years in prison and a $500,000 fine.

McMahon seemed to be spending more time in court than in wrestling arenas. On April 13, 1994, a federal jury in Minnesota awarded Jesse Ventura $809,958 in his lawsuit against the WWF for royalties on videotapes for which he had provided color commentary. Two weeks

As it grew in popularity and influence, the WWF was able to sign prominent wrestlers like Ric "Nature Boy" Flair, who left his long-time home with NWA/WCW in 1991.

later, Charles Austin, a preliminary wrestler paralyzed after a 1990 WWF tag team match in Tampa, was awarded $26.7 million in a lawsuit against the federation.

The eyes of the sports world were on the federal court in Uniondale, New York, when McMahon's trial started on July 5, 1994. Federal prosecutor Sean O'Shea accused McMahon of urging wrestlers to take steroids to make them more muscular, and thus more appealing to fans. Laura A. Brevetti, McMahon's attorney, replied that McMahon only told his wrestlers to be in shape, "steroids or no steroids."

Several wrestlers paraded to the witness stand to testify, including Tully Blanchard, Rick Rude, the Ultimate Warrior, and Hogan himself. Hogan's testimony was the most dramatic. Hogan admitted that he used steroids from 1976 to 1989, but denied that McMahon had told him or any other wrestler to use steroids. He did, however, say that he had used steroids with McMahon in 1988 in Atlanta while filming *No Holds Barred*. He testified that nearly 80 percent of WWF wrestlers used steroids when he was using them. Throughout his testimony, Hogan never made eye contact with McMahon.

The trial lasted two and a half weeks. On July 22 the jury came back with a verdict: not guilty. "I'm elated," McMahon told reporters. "Just like in wrestling, the good guys always win. I see nothing but blue skies ahead for the World Wrestling Federation."

Despite McMahon's happiness, storm clouds were, in fact, gathering. Ted Turner had become the WWF's fiercest rival. Turner, a billionaire who had bought Jim Crockett Promotions in 1988 and renamed it World Championship Wrestling (WCW), was tired of living in the WWF's promotional and financial shadows.

So while the WWF was busy fighting battles in court and on the public relations front, Turner made his move. In February 1993 Ric Flair returned to WCW. On June 11, three weeks before McMahon's trial began, WCW signed the biggest prize of all: Hulk Hogan.

"I can't say that that didn't hurt," McMahon told *Talk*. "I become very close to talent. I understand where they are coming from. When someone says, 'Gee, Vince, I'd love to stay, but Turner can pay me three times as much,' what can you do? But it still hurt."

In November, another former world champion, Randy Savage, also left the WWF and signed with WCW. For the first time in 10 years, the WWF wasn't the only major league promotion in professional wrestling.

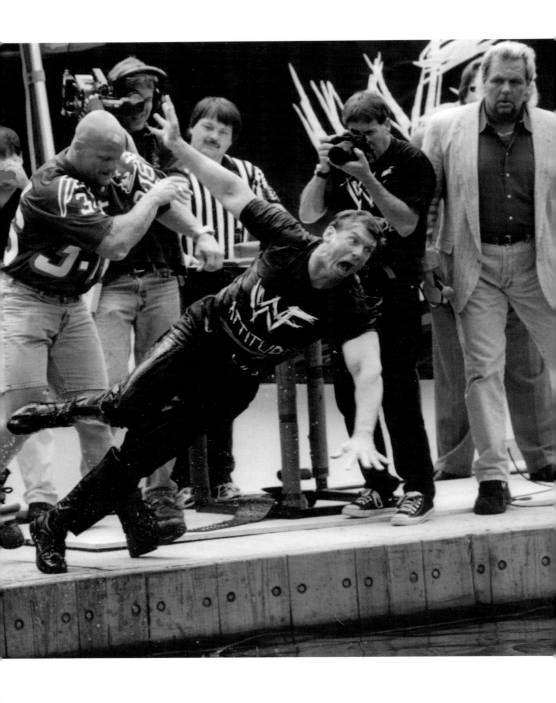

5 | THE FALL AND RISE OF THE WWF

For years the WWF had been recognized by the public, by wrestlers, and by the media as the world's leading wrestling federation. The WWF had it all: the most money, the largest roster of famous wrestlers, the biggest TV contracts, and the most-watched pay-per-view extravaganzas. WrestleMania, not Starrcade, was the biggest wrestling event of the year. SummerSlam, not WCW's Great American Bash, was the most anticipated card of the summer. The WWF had a monopoly on Monday-night cable-TV.

All that changed in 1995. WCW had become home to the best-known stars in wrestling: Randy Savage, Hulk Hogan, Lex Luger, Sting, the Giant, Ric Flair, "Diamond" Dallas Page, Brutus Beefcake, Hacksaw Duggan, and many others. The WWF, facing declining attendance and pay-per-view rates, and financially strapped from costly legal battles, couldn't compete with Turner, the billionaire cable-TV magnate who owned CNN and SuperStation TBS.

"They didn't just try to compete," McMahon told *Talk*. "They tried to put us out of business, and that's something different."

Of course, McMahon had tried to do the same thing to the NWA in 1987, when he had forced cable operators to choose between his Survivor Series and the NWA's Starrcade on

---

To boost the WWF's ratings, McMahon—shown being pushed into the water by "Stone Cold" Steve Austin—fostered feuds with his stars and resolved to get personally involved in the action.

Thanksgiving. In the early 1980s he was the reason numerous small federations went out of business. McMahon was finally getting a taste of his own medicine in a high-profile battle of egos: the millionaire McMahon vs. the billionaire Turner.

The WWF insisted that it was the choice of the "New Generation," with young wrestlers such as Razor Ramon, the Undertaker, Diesel, Sid Vicious, the Kid, Shawn Michaels, Savio Vega, Ahmed Johnson, and Hunter Hearst Helmsley. Steve Austin would sign on by the end of 1995, and Rocky Maivia—the Rock—would join the team in 1996. But WCW officials weren't concerned at all when Austin joined the WWF. He had been pushed out of WCW to make room for the superstars. He was one of their leftovers.

The WWF's "New Generation" marketing efforts were transparent. The truth was unavoidable: WCW had the big-name, big-money stars. The WWF, like a minor-league baseball team, had the stars of tomorrow, which didn't do much for them today.

About the only thing going for the WWF was its high ratings for *Monday Night Raw*, but that advantage diminished, too. In August 1995 the war between the federations intensified when WCW debuted *Monday Nitro* on TNT. The live show would go head-to-head with *Monday Night Raw*. If WCW really was trying to push the WWF out of business, now it was pushing harder.

The WWF impressed onlookers by holding a slight edge in the Monday night ratings war and seemed to be doing more with its young talent than WCW was doing with its famous, possibly overpriced talent. WCW was the home of glitz,

glamour, skits, and fireworks; the
WWF was the home of serious
wrestling.

Not that the WWF couldn't have
some fun once in a while. On the
January 1, 1996, *Raw*, for example,
a skit was shown depicting a WCW
board meeting. The characters were
the "Huckster," the "Nacho Man"
(a Randy Savage look-alike), and
"Billionaire Ted" (a Ted Turner look-
alike). The WWF poked fun at the
age of WCW's older stars.

McMahon, however, was losing
the war. In March 1996 former WWF
World champion Diesel announced that he was
leaving the WWF and going to WCW. Razor
Ramon, the four-time former WWF Intercontinental champion, followed closely behind.
McMahon could only watch as Diesel, wrestling
under his real name, Kevin Nash, and Ramon,
wrestling under his real name, Scott Hall, joined
with Hogan in WCW to form the New World
Order (NWO).

The NWO became a popular sensation, and
WCW totally eclipsed the WWF as the most-
watched wrestling federation in North America.
From late 1996 to early 1998, *Nitro* beat *Raw*
in the ratings war 83 weeks in a row. The
WWF's losses reached $6.5 million in 1997. The
WWF's TV contract with the USA Network was
in trouble. WCW vice president Eric Bischoff
boasted that the Monday night ratings war had
become boring.

"When I got to USA, they told me this tale of
how Turner had looked at the WWF, gotten
into the business, and stolen all the WWF's

In the 1990s, several prominent WWF stars—including Hulk Hogan—defected to WCW, where they boosted the ratings and popularity of that federation at the expense of the WWF.

people," USA Network head Barry Diller told *Talk.* "And I said, 'Wow, that's really terrible, but they've done it and they beat us.' What I really thought was, 'This is good, how quick can we get rid of this one?' But I was wrong. Vince McMahon is such a competitor that he plotted and he schemed and he figured out how to retake the franchise, and he did it. Left to my own devices, I would have killed the show."

McMahon's formula for regaining the throne was simple:

1. Give the young stars time to improve and develop their personalities.

2. Increase the amount of sex and violence in WWF programs.

3. Turn the federation into a soap opera.

4. Get personally involved in the action.

McMahon was fortunate to have Shawn Michaels, one of the most talented and charismatic wrestlers in the world, as his world champion. Michaels, with his good looks and arrogant style, helped maintain interest in the WWF. Mankind, formerly known as Cactus Jack, developed a cult following because of his no-holds-barred, hell-bent style of high-risk, high-impact wrestling. "Stone Cold" Steve Austin's political incorrectness was quickly gaining fans. When Jake Roberts, a Bible-thumping fan favorite with the motto "Jake 3:16," lost to Austin in the finals of the 1996 King of the Ring tournament, Austin told him in no uncertain terms what he thought about Jake 3:16. "You talk about your psalms, you talk about John 3:16. Well, Austin 3:16 says, 'I just whipped your [butt].'"

The next night, Stone Cold fans brought "Austin 3:16" banners to *Raw.* "Austin 3:16" became a catch-phrase in the WWF, emblazoned on countless signs and T-shirts. Suddenly, arrogance was hip. Wrestlers who in past years would have been considered rule-breakers because of their overbearing attitudes and obscenity-laced interviews had become fan favorites. Good was bad. Bad was good.

At SummerSlam on August 3, 1997, Austin pinned Owen Hart to capture the intercontinental title, even though he suffered a serious neck injury as the result of a piledriver by Hart. Doctors told Austin he had suffered acute spinal shock syndrome and had come within inches of being paralyzed for life.

Austin was in no condition to wrestle, and McMahon let him know it. When McMahon suggested that Austin be patient and work within the system, Austin used a "Stone-Cold stunner" on McMahon. The move is devastating: Technically, it's called a "three-quarter facelock bulldog." Physically, what happens is this: with an opponent's head positioned just above his shoulder, Austin reaches back and grabs his foe around the head, locking the head into his own shoulder. Often, Stone Cold will reach back with his other arm and link his hands together, further preventing his opponent from being able to escape. Next, Austin falls into a sit-down position on the mat, with the full force of the impact channeled through his own body and into his opponent's head.

At the Survivor Series on November 9, 1997, the stunner helped Austin regain the intercontinental title he lost when his injury left him unable to defend the belt.

McMahon was enraged. He considered Austin arrogant and disrespectful, but the fans loved Austin. He had shown incredible guts by returning to the ring despite a career-threatening injury. He had physically assaulted his boss, the man who signed his paychecks.

McMahon wasn't making many friends. Criticism was mounting in the media and among the fans about the way Vince had handled another important issue: Bret Hart's departure from the WWF.

The Canadian-born Hart, a five-time WWF World heavyweight champion, had been with the WWF since 1984 when his father, Stu Hart, sold the Stampede wrestling territory in Alberta, Canada, to McMahon. The two-time runner-up for *Pro Wrestling Illustrated*'s Wrestler of the Year was one of the best wrestlers in the world, and he was respected throughout the industry.

In 1996 Bret turned down a three-year, $9 million offer from WCW and signed a 20-year

Vince McMahon arm-wrestles Mankind while Sable referees. McMahon won the match—and his publicity war with WCW.

contract with the WWF. But, according to Hart's version of the story, in the fall of 1997 he received a call from McMahon, who said he wanted to break the contract. The WWF, facing mounting losses, couldn't afford Hart anymore. Stunned by the phone call, Hart called WCW to find out if their offer from a year ago was still good. It was. Hart accepted and gave notice to the WWF.

The problem was that Hart was the WWF World champion, having won the belt from the Undertaker at SummerSlam '97. McMahon had no intention of allowing Hart to leave for WCW with the WWF World title belt strapped around his waist. Prior to Hart's Survivor Series showdown with Michaels on November 9, 1997, McMahon told Hart to lay down and lose the match on purpose.

Hart, however, considered himself to be a man of integrity and had no desire to lose on purpose. And the Survivor Series was being held in Montreal, Canada—Hart's home country, where he is considered a hero. He thought it would be humiliating to lose the belt in front of his own fans.

According to Hart, McMahon had given him his word that there would be no monkey business in the match. But three seconds after Michaels locked Hart in a sharpshooter, referee Earl Hebner called for the bell and declared that Hart had submitted. Hart, who clearly had never submitted, was enraged. He stormed back to the dressing room and, according to witnesses, punched McMahon several times.

"What he did with me in the Survivor Series was a total lack of respect for my fans, my fellow wrestlers, and me," Hart said. "I worked

14 years and gave this man the greatest performances in the history of the game, having missed only two shows in 14 years, having been a leader inside and outside the dressing room. And for Vince McMahon to lie to me and cheat me for no other reason at all other than his own paranoid delusions shows what kind of a man he really is."

McMahon had no time for debates. He still had Austin to worry about.

At the D-Generation X pay-per-view on December 7, 1997, Austin drove his truck to the ring for a match against Rocky Maivia, also known as the Rock. The next night at *Raw*, McMahon berated Austin for using his truck as a weapon and ordered him to defend the title against the Rock. When Austin walked outside and tossed the belt into a river, McMahon named Maivia the new champion.

Austin set his sights on winning the WWF World heavyweight title, and McMahon set his sights on denying Austin what he wanted. Austin won the Royal Rumble to earn a shot against champion Shawn Michaels at Wrestle-Mania XIV on March 29, 1988. Mike Tyson was named special referee. A few days before the event, McMahon publicly declared, "Austin as world champion would be a public relations and promotional nightmare" for the federation.

At WrestleMania XIV, Austin defeated Michaels to win the WWF World heavyweight championship.

Immediately, McMahon set out to mold Austin into his idea of a corporate champion. At *Raw* the day after WrestleMania, McMahon called out Austin, who was wearing a suit and a tie. McMahon told Austin that he wanted him to carry the WWF into the next millennium as its corporate champion. Austin responded by giving McMahon another stone cold stunner.

At Unforgiven on April 26, Austin clobbered McMahon with a chair during his match against Dude Love. McMahon was carried off on a stretcher. McMahon accepted Austin's challenge for a head-to-head match at *Raw*. The fans in Philadelphia that night chanted, "Vince is dead! Vince is dead!" Dude Love interfered before the match started.

McMahon did everything in his power to foil Austin. He named himself outside-the-ring referee for the Austin vs. Hunter Hearst Helmsley match on May 23 in Toronto. Although McMahon interfered, Austin pinned Helmsley to retain the title.

McMahon dipped further into his bag of tricks. He refereed another Austin vs. Love match at the Over the Edge pay-per-view event on May 31, 1998, and named associates Pat Patterson and Jerry Brisco as guest announcer and guest timekeeper. Austin won again.

Though Austin was winning the matches, McMahon was the winner in terms of business. Sales of Austin merchandise were booming. *Raw*'s ratings were surging. Thanks to the McMahon vs. Austin feud, *Raw* was once again beating *Nitro* in the Monday night ratings war. In late May of 1998 the USA Network renewed its contract with the WWF.

Vince McMahon was about to become one of the richest men in all of sports.

6   A FAMILY AFFAIR

For years, he was known as Vince McMahon, the behind-the-scenes owner of the WWF who stepped in front of the curtain to become the federation's TV play-by-play man, too. But in 1998 Vince McMahon became Mr. McMahon, the seemingly insane, power-hungry boss who hatched one plot after another to strip "Stone Cold" Steve Austin of the world title.

Mr. McMahon was a major star.

McMahon's hatred for Austin intensified by the day. He convinced Kane to set himself on fire if Kane lost a "first blood" match to Austin at the King of the Ring pay-per-view on June 28, 1998. Kane beat Austin and won the world title, but lost it back to Austin the following night, further enraging McMahon. When Austin retained the title with a victory over the Undertaker at SummerSlam '98, McMahon stepped up his efforts to get Austin. He scheduled Austin for a series of three-way matches involving Kane and the Undertaker.

"I guarantee you Steve Austin will no longer be WWF World champion after September 27, 1998," vowed McMahon, who refused to reveal his master plan.

Right on schedule, on September 27, 1998, at Copps Coliseum in Hamilton, Ontario, Canada, Austin was simultaneously pinned by Kane and the Undertaker and lost the title.

Thanks to feuds and alliances with some of the federation's most popular wrestlers, audiences saw more and more of Vince McMahon and family, who were drawn into the plot lines of the WWF.

A day later, McMahon ordered a match between Kane and the Undertaker to decide the world champion. Austin would be the referee.

"And if you don't make a three-count and raise one of their hands as champion, I will fire you," McMahon told Austin.

Austin was defiant. He laid out Kane and the Undertaker, and made three-counts on both of them. He declared himself champion. McMahon, true to his word, fired Stone Cold, but a new adversary was ready and willing to

Siblings Shane and Stephanie McMahon are the fourth generation of McMahons to be involved in professional wrestling, and in recent years they have expanded their involvement with the WWF.

take the place of Austin: his own son, Shane McMahon.

At the time, Shane was working behind the scenes as a WWF executive. As a man with a financial stake in the WWF, he was concerned that his father was trying to oust the most popular man in the federation, the man who was generating the most revenue. He exercised his corporate power and reinstated Austin.

Austin shouldn't have been fooled. Shane refereed Austin's match against Mankind in the second round of the world title tournament at the 1998 Survivor Series. Austin had Mankind covered for the pin, but Shane stopped counting at two. Gerald Brisco, one of McMahon's henchmen, flattened Austin with a chair, allowing Mankind to score the pin. That night, Vince, Shane, Pat Patterson, and WWF commissioner Sergeant Slaughter made sure Rocky Maivia won the world title tournament.

"There's only one person who hates the fans more than the McMahons," Maivia told *Pro Wrestling Illustrated Weekly*, "and that's 'the Rock.' Now Mr. McMahon has a champion he can be proud of—the best damn world champion the WWF ever had."

The WWF now had three major stars: Austin, the Rock, and McMahon. *Raw*'s ratings soared. The WWF had become a national sensation. McMahon's Team Corporate was Public Enemy No. 1.

McMahon entered himself into the 1999 Royal Rumble, then made sure he'd be the last person into the ring and Austin would be the first. Austin and McMahon were the only two men remaining when Austin knocked out McMahon. Austin was about to dump McMahon over the top rope to win the match when the Rock distracted Austin. McMahon snuck up behind Austin, tossed him over the top rope for the win, and became the number one contender to the world title.

The showdown that Austin and the rest of the wrestling world had been waiting for took place on February 14, 1999, at the St. Valentine's Day Massacre pay-per-view: Austin vs. McMahon in a steel cage match. McMahon claimed he had a foolproof plan for beating Austin, but Austin was no fool. He tossed McMahon around the ring like a rag doll. He pushed McMahon off the cage and sent him crashing through the broadcasters' table. McMahon was carried away on a stretcher.

McMahon enlisted help from Paul Wight, the 7' 2" federation newcomer who had previously wrestled in WCW as the Giant, and would become known in the WWF as the Big Show. At WrestleMania XV on March 28, 1999, at First Union Center in Philadelphia, Austin was scheduled to battle the Rock for the world title. The referee for the match would be the winner of the Wight vs. Mankind match earlier in the evening.

During that earlier match, Wight was disqualified for choke-slamming Mankind through two metal chairs. Mankind couldn't referee the match because of the injuries he suffered at the hands of Wight. McMahon tried to declare himself referee for the title match, but WWF commissioner Shawn Michaels, citing WWF rules, barred McMahon from the ring. McMahon tried to interfere anyway, but Mankind hobbled back to the ring and counted Austin's pin of the Rock.

By this time, Vince had other things to worry about. Shane, who had proven his wrestling ability by winning the WWF European title, had set out to wrest control of the federation from his father. At *Raw* on April 19, 1999 Shawn slapped his father across the face, signifying his independence from Vince. He went on to gain control of the Corporation, and combined with the Undertaker to form the Corporate Ministry.

At the Backlash pay-per-view, Shane refereed the world title match between Austin and the Rock. With 20 minutes gone in the bout, Austin went for the pin, but Shane refused to make the count. Vince came out and ordered referee Earl Hebner to finish the match. As Vince battled his son at ringside, Austin pinned the Rock.

But Austin had every reason to be wary. Months later, the power behind the Corporate Ministry was revealed to be McMahon. Austin still had some friends in the McMahon family though: Linda, Vince's wife, and Stephanie, their youngest child, battled with Shane and Vince over control of the federation. Linda and Stephanie named Austin CEO of the WWF. But when Shane and Vince beat Austin in a handicap ladder match at the June 27, 1999, King of the Ring, held in Greensboro, North Carolina, Austin had to relinquish his position.

Austin fired back. At the Fully Loaded pay-per-view on July 25, he beat the Undertaker. As a result of Austin's victory, Vince McMahon was banned from the WWF.

With Vince gone, the spotlight shined on Stephanie. During the Summer of 1999, Stephanie started dating the wrestler Test. Vince was opposed to the pairing, but Stephanie seemed to be smitten. Finally, with Shane and Vince's approval, Stephanie and Test set a wedding date.

A few months later, Austin allowed Vince to return to the federation as owner. He and Austin formed another shaky alliance built around Austin's feud with WWF champion Triple-H. Vince managed to get the belt away from Triple-H in a three-way match at the 1999 Survivor Series. Triple-H was enraged.

Meanwhile, Stephanie and Test were scheduled to get married at *Raw* on November 29, 1999. Triple-H crashed the wedding, then showed a video of himself marrying a seemingly drunk Stephanie at a drive-through chapel in Las Vegas. Stephanie burst into tears. Vince screamed angrily at Triple-H, who got in the last word. He called Vince, "Dad."

Two weeks later, Triple-H beat Vince in a no-holds-barred match at the Armageddon pay-per-view. While Vince lay motionless in the middle of the ring, Stephanie shocked the wrestling world by embracing her new husband.

"It makes me think that Stephanie's engagement to Test was a ruse from the very start," said WWF announcer Jim Ross.

Devastated by his daughter's marriage to Triple-H, Vince disappeared from the federation for several months. Meanwhile, Stephanie and Triple-H took over the WWF. They ordered their enemies, particularly the Rock, to compete in one-sided handicap matches. The McMahon-Helmsley Era had begun.

But Shane wanted to end it as quickly as possible. He returned at the No Way Out pay-per-view on February 27, 2000, and helped the Big Show defeat the Rock. A month later, during a match between the Rock and Big Show at *Raw*, Vince returned, nailed special referee Shane with a chair, and counted the Rock's pin of Big Show.

Vince took command.

"You don't run the federation," he told Stephanie and Triple-H. "I do."

Vince ruled that the main event of WrestleMania would be Triple-H vs. the Rock vs. the Big Show. Shane would stand in Big Show's corner. Stephanie

Hunter Hearst Helmsley reacts after defeating the Rock at WrestleMania 2000, inaugurating the McMahon-Helmsley era of the WWF.

would be in Triple-H's corner. Vince would be in the Rock's corner. A few days later, Linda added her own twist to the match: Mick Foley, who had recently retired, would compete in the WrestleMania main event, and she would be in his corner.

The "fatal four-way match" at WrestleMania was the most highly anticipated match of the year. Late in the contest, the Rock and Triple-H were the only two men remaining. With over 26 minutes gone, Vince interfered on the Rock's behalf. Shane came back to the ring and nailed his father with a TV monitor. Vince and Shane battled as the Rock and Triple-H lay motionless in the ring. Bloodied, Vince was helped back to the locker room. The Rock got up and DDT'd Triple-H for a two-count. Shane got ready to hit the Rock with a chair, but the Rock slingshotted Triple-H into the chair. The Rock clobbered

Triple-H and prepared to score the pin. Vince returned to the ring and nailed Shane. But then, Vince chaired the Rock. Triple-H covered the Rock for the pin. Vince and Shane embraced.

The McMahon-Helmsley regime was bigger and stronger than ever. The Rock seemed to be fighting a losing battle against the powerful owners, but he fought gallantly and won the world title. The McMahon family was split, with Shane, Vince, and Stephanie on one side, and Linda on the other.

At the beginning of the new millennium the McMahon family had become the most powerful, controversial, and colorful family in wrestling. It had also become the most successful.

Raw Is War, now on TNN, is the number one show on cable TV. According to *Fortune* magazine, the WWF is worth $850 million, and Vince's personal fortune had reached the $1.1 billion mark. In 1999 the WWF became a publicly-traded company on the New York Stock Exchange. In three years, the WWF's annual revenues went from $82 million to $379 million. Shane oversees the website WWF.com, which in late 2000 attracted nearly two million visitors a month. Early in 2000, Vince McMahon announced plans to launch a new professional football league, the XFL.

WWF wrestlers, such as the Rock, Triple-H, and Austin have appeared on the covers of national magazines such as *TV Guide* and *Entertainment Weekly*. The WWF has created a multimillion dollar business selling T-shirts, video games, and action figures. Mankind's biography, *Have a Nice Day*, went to number

Vince McMahon announces plans for a new professional football league known as the XFL at a February 2000 press conference in New York. The proposed XFL will have eight teams and will begin playing after the end of the traditional football season.

one on the *New York Times* bestseller list. In contrast, by early 2001 media mogul Ted Turner had decided to sell WCW, which was losing the ratings war to WWF.

Throughout its massive success, the WWF has not been above criticism. Several TV critics and watchdog groups have accused WWF programming of being too filled with violence and sexual content. But McMahon has an answer for his critics.

"My job is to entertain the masses at whatever level they want," he told *U.S. News and World Report.*

He has always done his job. It's likely that he will continue to do so for a long, long time to come.

Chronology

1925 Madison Square Garden in New York opens. Jesse McMahon promotes the first boxing match at the arena

1935 Vince McMahon Sr. promotes his first wrestling card

1945 Vincent Kennedy McMahon Jr. is born in Pinehurst, North Carolina, on August 24

1963 Vince McMahon Sr. separates from the NWA and forms the WWWF

1966 Vince McMahon Jr. marries Linda, his childhood sweetheart

1971 Vince Sr. makes his son head of Capitol Wrestling's operations in Maine

1982 Vince Jr. and Linda buy Capitol Wrestling from Vince McMahon Sr.

1984 Hulk Hogan wins the world title from the Iron Sheik—"Hulkamania" is born on January 23; Vince McMahon Sr. dies on May 27

1985 The first WrestleMania is held at Madison Square Garden on March 31

1986 WrestleMania II takes place in Chicago, Long Island, and Los Angeles on April 7

1988 On October 17, *Forbes* magazine reports that the WWF is worth $100 million

1992 The WWF is hit by allegations of sexual misconduct and steroid abuse

1993 A federal grand jury indicts McMahon and Titan Sports on charges of possession of anabolic steroids and conspiracy to distribute steroids

1994 Hulk Hogan signs with WCW on June 11; on July 22 McMahon is acquitted of all charges of conspiracy to distribute steroids

1997 Losing its battle with WCW, the WWF's annual losses are $6.5 million; McMahon begins his feud with Steve Austin

1998 McMahon's war with Austin intensifies and the WWF's *Monday Night Raw* passes WCW's *Monday Nitro* in the Monday night ratings battle

1999 Vince's children, Shane and Stephanie, get involved in WWF feuds, along with Linda; the WWF becomes a publicly traded company on October 18

2000 *Fortune* estimates that the WWF is worth $850 million; the WWF announces the formation of a new pro football league called the XFL

Further Reading

Burkett, Harry. "Wrestle-McMania! Power . . . Greed . . Pride." *Pro Wrestling Illustrated* (September 2000): 19–21.

Foley, Mick. Mankind: *Have a Nice Day! A Tale of Blood and Sweatsocks.* New York: Regan Books/Harper Collins, 1999.

Rosellini, Lynn. "Lords of the Ring." *U.S. News and World Report* (17 May 1999): 52–58.

Smith, Richard. "Money Mania." *Audacity* (Summer 1993): 22–31.

Surowiecki, James. "Good, Clean, Family Money." *Talk* (October 1999): 186–217.

Zabriskie, Phillip. "The Icon Profile: Vince McMahon." *Icon* (August 1997): 76–81.

Index

Photo Credits

Associated Press/WWP: pp. 12, 23, 28, 34, 38, 40; Blackjack Brown: p. 17; Corbis/Bettmann: p. 20; Jeff Eisenberg Sports Photography: pp. 2, 6, 9, 32, 37, 46, 50, 52, 59; Howard Kernats Photography: p. 57; Sports Action: pp. 43, 60.

KYLE ALEXANDER has been involved in the publication of professional wrestling magazines for more than a decade. His previously published volumes about professional wrestling include *The Story of the Wrestler They Call " Sting"* and *Bill Goldberg.* Over the past 10 years, he has made numerous appearances on radio and television, offering his unique perspective on the "sport of kings."